Phonics

Pictures and Word Cards!

Hundreds of reproducible illustrations and matching word cards!

By Karen Sevaly

boat

hammer

pig

Teacher's Friend,
A Scholastic Company

Permission to Reproduce

Phonics Pictures and Word Cards!

Printed in China.

ISBN-13 978-0-439-89306-0
ISBN-10 0-439-89306-2

Cover design and illustrations: Karen Sevaly
Graphic Layout: Susan Isaacs

Table of Contents

Making the Most of This Book

This Phonics Picture Book contains hundreds of delightful, reproducible illustrations for teaching phonemic awareness and emergent reading skills. Each illustration comes with a matching word card. Numerous learning activities and games can be made with the illustrations, word cards, and letter cards contained in this book. Here are a few suggestions:

Letter of the Day/Week

Display a large, cut-out letter on the class board. Enlarge the illustrations and post them and the matching words that start with that letter around the board. Ask the children to compare other letters they have learned with the letter of the day.

Give each child five or six illustrations and the matching word cards. Ask them to paste the pictures with the matching words to a sheet of construction paper. Provide a place for each child to practice tracing and writing the letter of the day.

Picture-Word Match

Select several beginning letter sounds you want the students to practice. Copy and cut several illustrations for each letter and paste them on 3"X5" cards. Do the same with the matching letter cards (page 91.) Place the cards on a tabletop and have students match the pictures to the appropriate letter card.

Concentration Match

Beginning with 10 letters or less, select two illustrations for each letter. Copy, cut and then paste each illustration on a 3"X5" card. To play the game, place all of the cards facedown. The first player then chooses two cards to turn over. If the beginning sounds of the illustrations match, he or she keeps the pair and takes another turn. If the cards do not match, then the next player gets a turn. The students must use visual memory skills to try and remember the location of the matching letter-sound pairs. The student with the most matched pairs wins the game.

Alphabet Bingo

Make each child a copy of the Bingo card pattern on page 96. Select one illustration representing the beginning sound for each letter and enlarge it on a copy machine. Include both consonants and beginning vowels. Ask each student to write a different letter in the squares of their Bingo card. (Tell them to make sure to not write the letters in alphabetical order, but rather place the letters randomly on the card.) Pull one of the letter illustrations and hold it up for each player to see. Ask them to determine the beginning letter sound and then to circle that letter on their card. Continue playing until one player gets a BINGO!

Alphabet Board Game

Make your own simple gameboard and paste it to colorful paper. Copy, cut and paste a beginning-sound illustration to each space on the game board. Two to four students can play. The first player rolls a die and moves the designated number of spaces. He or she must then tell the beginning sound (letter) of the picture. If correct, he/she remains on that square. If incorrect, he/she must move back to the previous position. Play continues with all players until someone reaches the "finish" line first and wins the game.

Bb

Bb

Bb Words

baby	bird
ball	boat
balloon	bone
bat	book
bear	bow
bed	boy
bee	bug
bell	bus
bike	butterfly

Cc

Cc

Cc Words

cactus	carrot
cake	cat
camel	coat
can	comb
candle	cook
candy	corn
cane	cow
canoe	cowboy
car	cup

Dd
THE UNITED STATES OF AMERICA
ONE DOLLAR

LIBERTY
Dd

Dd Words

deer	dollar
desk	door
dice	doughnut
dime	down
dinosaur	dress
dishes	drum
dog	duck
doll	

Ff

Ff
FD

Ff Words

fan	flag
feather	flower
fence	feet
fire	football
fireman	fork
finger	fox
fish	frog
five	fruit

Gg

GUM
Gg

Gg Words

game	glove
gate	glue
ghost	goat
gift	goose
gingerbread man	grapes
giraffe	grasshopper
girl	guitar
glass	gum

Hh

Hh

Hh Words

ham	hippo
hammer	hive
hand	hook
hat	horn
hay	horse
heart	hose
helicopter	hot dog
hen	house

Jj

 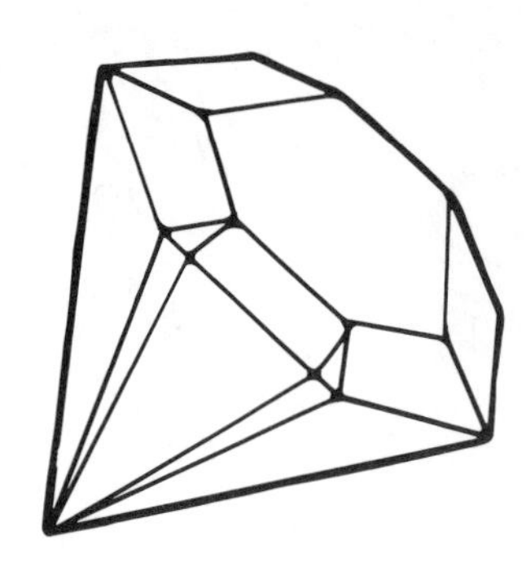  

Jj Words

jacket	jar
jack-in-the-box	jeep
jack-o'-lantern	jellyfish
jacks	jewel
jam	jug

Kk

Kk Words

kangaroo	kiss
kettle	kitchen
key	kite
kick	kitten
king	koala

Ll

Ll
Dear Maria,
I hope you can
come soon. I
really miss you.
We can plan a
picnic and a
trip to the zoo.
Let me know the
1

Ll Words

ladder	letter
ladybug	light
lamb	lightning
lamp	lion
leaf	lips
leg	lock
lemon	log
leprechaun	

Mm
THE UNITED STATES OF AMERICA
THE UNITED STATES OF AMERICA
ONE DOLLAR
MILK

Mm
MILK

Mm Words

mailbox	mitten
man	money
map	monkey
mask	moon
match	mop
mice	mouse
milk	mouth
mitt	mushroom

Nn
The Press
2 3 8 6 5 7 4
IN GOD WE TRUST
LIBERTY
1967
9

Nn
Please take out the trash.

Nn Words

nail	nine
neck	nose
necklace	note
needle	numbers
nest	nurse
net	nuts
newspaper	
nickel	

Pp
PAINT

Pp

Pp Words

pail	pie
paint	pig
pan	pillow
pear	pizza
pen	pool
pencil	popcorn
penguin	pumpkin
piano	puzzle

Qq
UNITED STATES OF AMERICA
QUARTER DOLLAR
Shh...

Qq Words

quack	question mark
quail	quiet
quarter	quilt
queen	

Rr

Rr
31

Rr Words

rabbit	reindeer
raccoon	ring
race car	rock
radio	rocket
rain	rooster
rake	rope
rattle	rose
refrigerator	rug

Ss
SOAP

Ss

Ss Words

sailboat	snake
sandwich	snowflake
saw	snowman
seahorse	soap
seal	sock
sink	spider
skate	squirrel
sled	sun

Tt

Tt

Tt Words

table	toothbrush
tape	top
teeth	train
telephone	tree
television	truck
tent	tub
tie	turkey
tiger	turtle

Vv
ELECTION
Be Mine!

Vv Words

vacuum	vest
valentine	vine
van	violin
vase	volcano
vegetables	vote

Ww

Ww

Ww Words

wagon	whistle
walrus	wig
watch	windmill
watermelon	window
wave	wing
web	witch
well	woman
wheel	worm

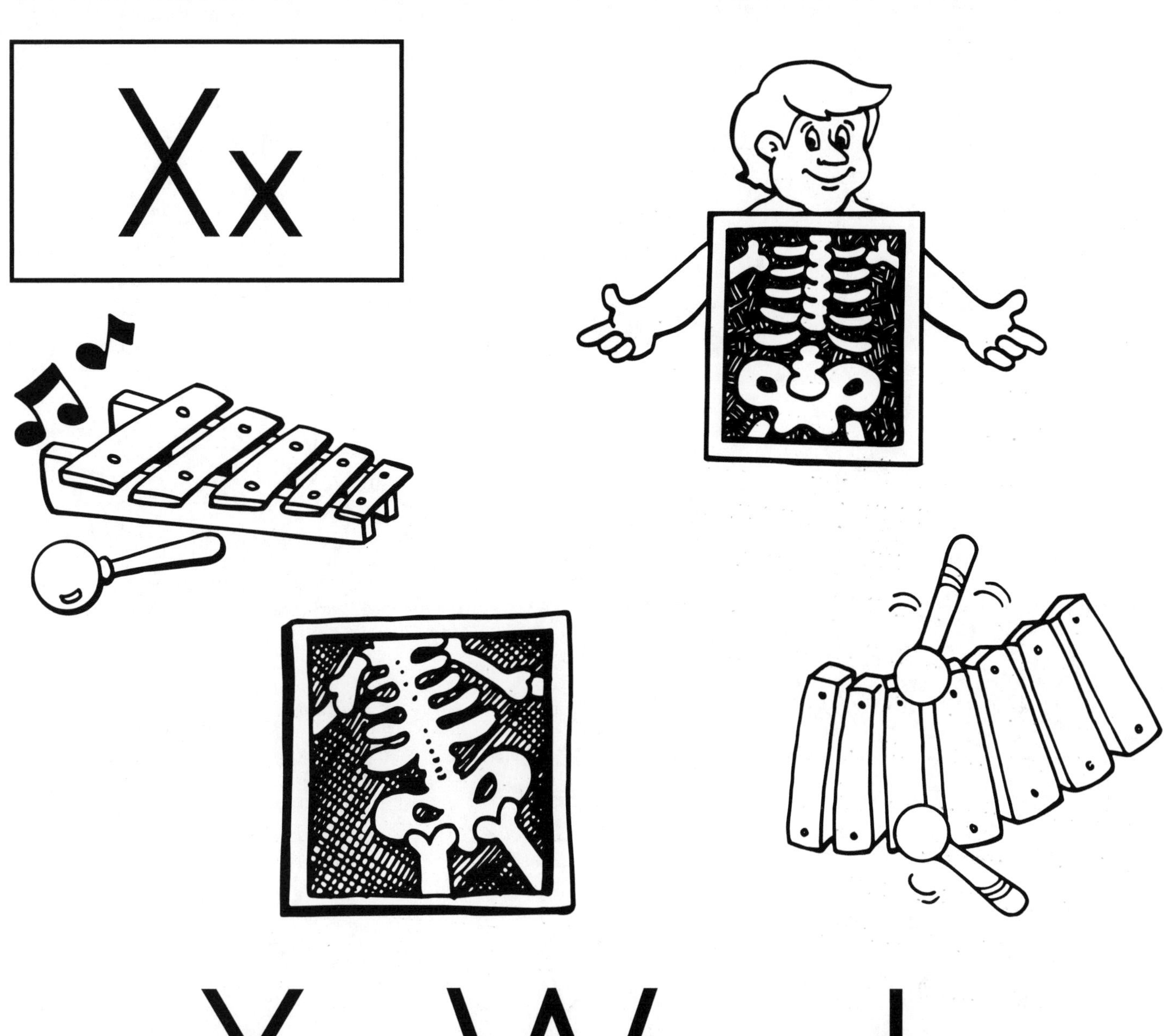

Xx Words

x-ray	xylophone

Yy
YOYO
YARN
Yellow
Yellow

Yy Words

yak	yellow
yarn	yolk
yawn	yo-yo

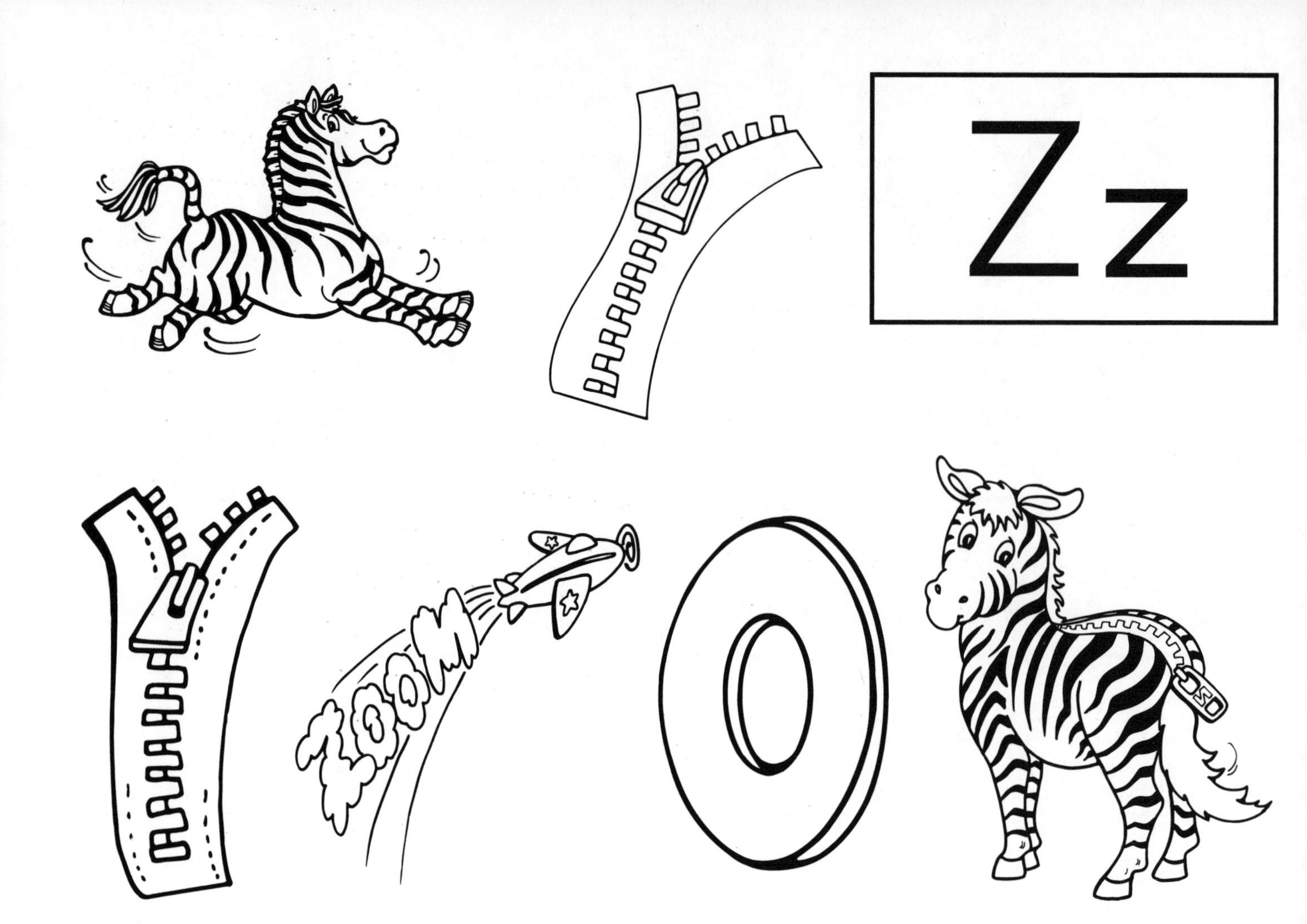

Zz Words

zebra	zipper
zero	zoom

Aā
PAINT

Aā

Aā Words

acorn	rain
cake	rake
cane	skate
chain	snail
grapes	tape
hay	train
pail	vase
paint	whale

Eē

Eē

Eē Words

bee	queen
cheese	seal
eagle	sheep
eel	teeth
jeep	tree
key	wheel
leaf	wreath
peas	zebra

I ī

Iī
LIBERTY

Iī Words

bike	kite
dime	light
fire	lion
five	mice
hive	pie
ice	tie
ice cream	
iron	

Oō
SOAP

Oo

Oō Words

boat	phone
bone	pillow
bow	rope
coat	rose
comb	soap
ghost	snowman
goat	snowflake
hose	window

Uū
(y̅o̅o̅)
Dessert

Uū Words

bugle	ruler
cube	unicorn
menu	uniform
mule	United States
music	

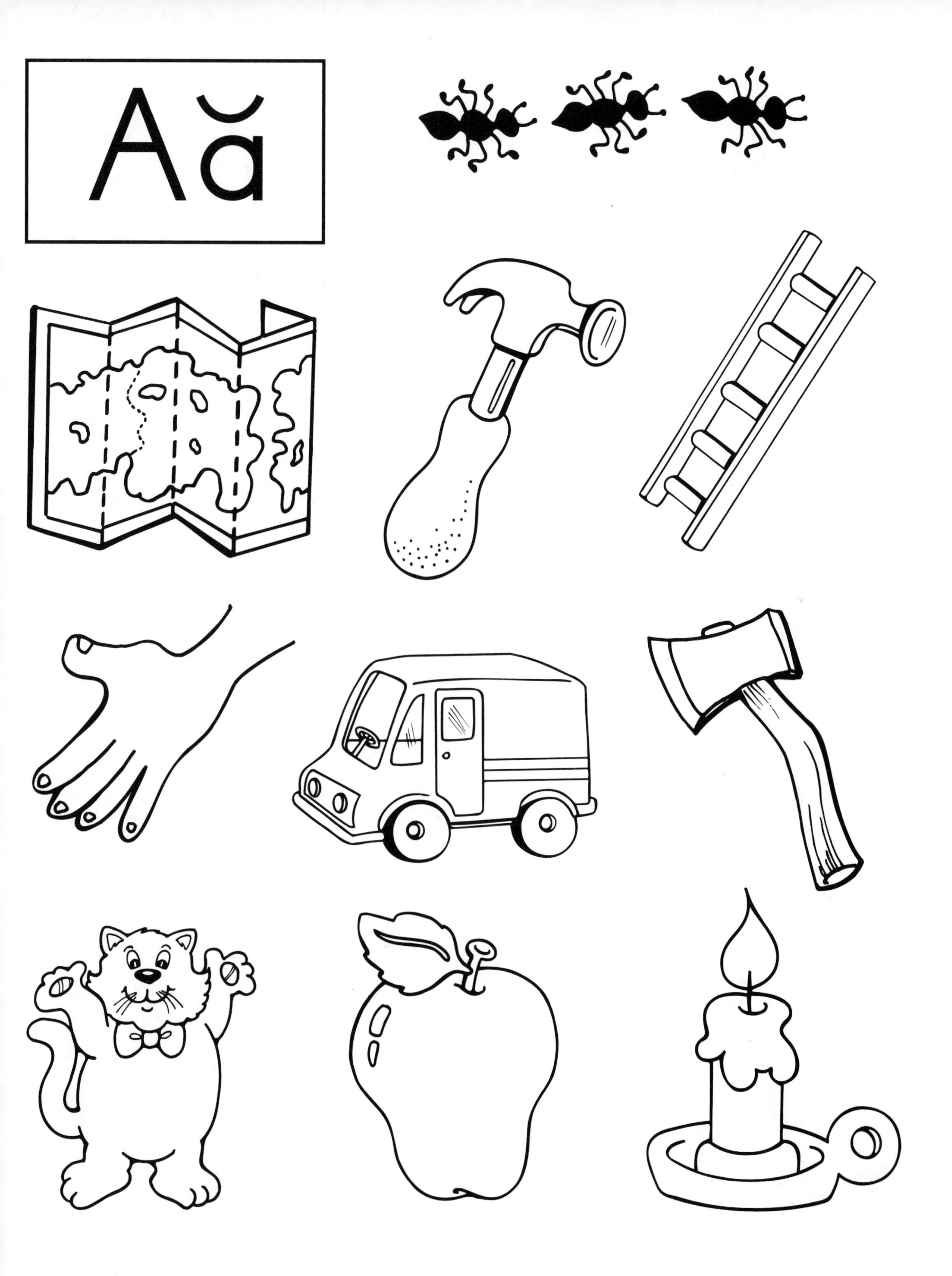
Aă

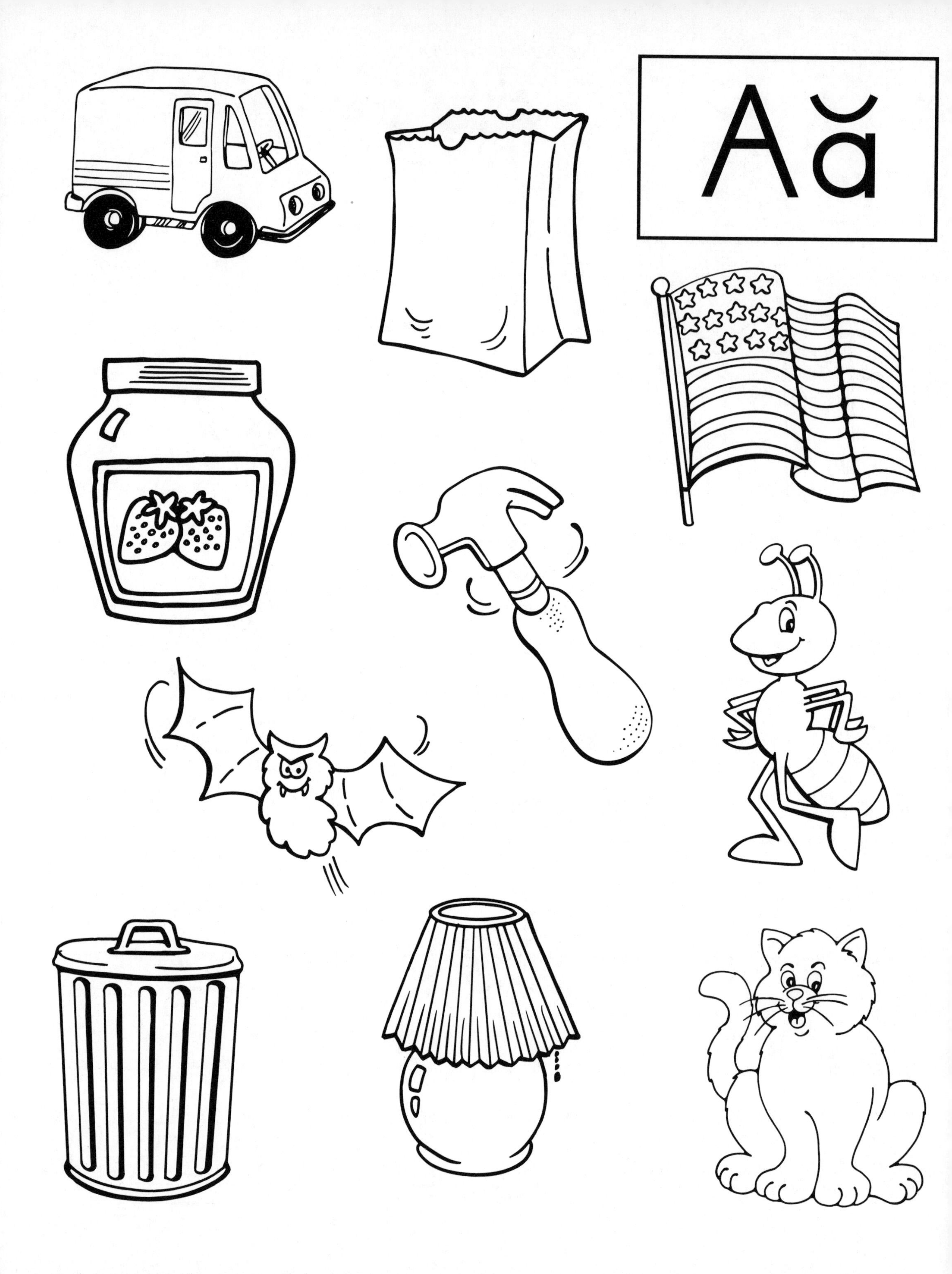

Aă

Aă Words

ant	flag
apple	hammer
ax	hand
bag	jam
bat	ladder
can	lamp
candle	map
cat	van

Eĕ
Red

E ĕ
Dear Maria,
I hope you can
come soon. I
really miss you.
We can plan a
picnic and a
trip to the zoo.
Let me know the

Eĕ Words

bed	nest
bell	net
desk	red
egg	shell
elephant	sled
elf	tent
hen	vest
letter	well

Iĭ

Iĭ
MILK

Iĭ Words

dishes	milk
fish	mitt
gift	mittens
igloo	pig
ink	sink
insects	six
kick	wig
lizard	zipper

Oo
D C
S T
A L
12
1
2
3
4
5
6
7
8
9
10
11
STOP

Oŏ
12
1
2
3
4
5
6
7
8
9
10
11

Oŏ Words

blocks	log
box	octopus
clock	ostrich
dog	popcorn
doll	rock
fox	rocket
frog	socks
lock	stop

Uŭ
GUM

U ŭ
SCHOOL

Uŭ Words

brush	nuts
bus	pumpkin
cup	rug
drum	skunk
duck	truck
gum	tub
jug	umbrella
jump	up

oo

o͝o

o͞o Words

balloon	kangaroo
broom	moon
goose	school
igloo	spoon

o͝o Words

book	foot
cook	football
cookie	hook

Alphabet Cards
Capital Letters

A	B	C
D	E	F
G	H	I
J	K	L

M	N	O
P	Q	R
S	T	U
V	W	X
Y	Z	

Alphabet Cards
Lowercase Letters

a	b	c
d	e	f
g	h	i
j	k	l

m	n	o
p	q	r
s	t	u
v	w	x
y	z	

Alphabet Cards
Long and Short Vowels

ā	ū	ŏ
ē	ă	ŭ
ī	ĕ	o͞o
ō	ĭ	o͝o

Name ______________________

BINGO

B	I	N	G	O
		FREE		